CLEAR YOUR HEAD

the guide to enjoying your life
without anxiety getting in the way

Tim Box

Published in Great Britain in 2017
Under the **HypnoArts™** label by
the Academy of Hypnotic Arts ltd.
1 Emperor Way, Exeter, EX13QS
Tel: +44 1392 314090
AcademyofHypnoticArts.com

Enquiries should be addressed to the
Academy of Hypnotic Arts
bookpub@hypnoarts.com

First printed edition 2017
British Library Cataloguing in Publication Data
ISBN Number: 978-1-9997641-3-5

For my parents who raised me happy.
For Britt who keeps me happy.
All my love always.

CONTENTS

A special note about how this book was created

This book was originally created as a live interview. That's why it reads as a conversation rather than a traditional book that talks "at you". It's also why it isn't after an award for literature but, it will engage, educate and empower you

I wanted you to feel as though I am talking "with you", much like a close friend or relative. I felt that creating the material this way would make it easier for you to grasp the topics and put them to use quickly, rather than wading through hundreds of heavily edited pages.

So relax, and get ready to know how to enjoy your life without anxiety getting in the way so you can understand that anxiety can be your friend, not your enemy!

Let's get started and

Clear Your Head right now...

Sincerely, *Tim Box*

Meet Tim Box

Tim Box is a hands-on expert on the subject of anxiety control, and has graciously consented to this interview to share with us the advice, techniques, and strategies every anxiety sufferer can and must develop in order to know how to enjoy your life without anxiety getting in the way.

Tim's had a grammar school education. He studied English literature and philosophy at Kent University. He's a registered advanced hypnotist, holds a hypnotherapy practitioner diploma and a diploma in clinical advanced hypnotherapy.

He's had seven years running a full-time remedial hypnosis practise and runs one-day CONTROL workshops for anxiety sufferers.

Tim is a fellow of the Academy of Hypnotic Arts and a member of the National Council for Hypnotherapy.

He's spoken and trained at BNI, that's Business

Network International, at their national conference and he won Complementary Health Practitioner of the Year at the Kent Health and Beauty Awards, both in 2016.

In 2015, he developed his CONTROL System, making changes in patterns of thought.

If you're an anxiety sufferer, most of what you need is instruction and encouragement from someone who's been there and done that, with how to enjoy your life without anxiety getting in your way.

As you can see, anxiety control expert Tim Box is uniquely qualified to help you understand everything you need to know about getting control of anxiety, without drugs in the vast majority of cases.

Introduction

Jon: Hi, everyone, and welcome to Clear
       Your Head, especially for anxiety
       sufferers.

       As with all of our expert's works, if you
       want to enhance your experience of life,
       then there will be advice and techniques
       you should know and will benefit from
       whether you're an anxiety sufferer or
       not.

       My name is Jon Chase, and today I'm
       talking with anxiety control expert Tim
       Box about what all anxiety sufferers
       need to have to be successful with
       anxiety control and get the best results.

What is Clear Your Head?

Jon: Welcome, Tim.

Tim: Hello, Jon.

Jon: Let's just jump right in with a quick
         summary explanation. Tim, in a short
         sentence or two, what is *Clear Your
         Head?*

Tim: Clear Your Head is a way of thinking or
         understanding how the mind works; it
         shows you how to enjoy your life
         without anxiety getting in the way.

         When you understand how this works
         and you understand how your mind's
         working, you'll be able to sleep well,
         increase your self-esteem and your
         confidence levels and basically clear
         your head.

Tim's Story

Jon: Tim, tell us, how did you get here?

Tim: Originally, back when I left university
       having studied philosophy, I left to join
       a band and I was a bit of a punk rocker
       for a bit. During that time, I had to do
       something to pay the bills, so I became
       a plumber.

       The reason I bring this into my story is
       because one of the side effects of doing
       plumbing was that I learned to have a
       general good level of rapport with
       people.

       When I went into plumbing, I had a fair
       amount of social anxiety. Even though I
       would be on stage playing to...
       sometimes thousands of people if I was
       lucky, sometimes two people and a dog,

but no matter how many people there were, I had that wall of sound behind me that was protecting me.

When it came to actually engaging in one-on-one conversations, I was not good at it and I would shy away from it at every opportunity.

What becoming a plumber did was had me go into people's houses, talking to them, having to gain their trust.

Around that time, everything on the TV was about rogue traders and how all the tradesmen were going to rip you off.

All I was doing, I was just in my dad's company, I was helping him out and he was spending the last 10 years of his working life back on the tools.

Then it came that time when he said, "Okay. I'm going to retire now. How about I give you the plumbing company?"

I thought, "Whoa. Hang on a minute. Am I going to be a plumber the rest of my life?"

Coming from an academic and an artistic and creative background, that wasn't what I wanted to be.

Just to clarify, I was a very *specific* type of plumber: I was a *shit* plumber.

It wasn't my calling at all.

Basically I needed to find something else. It was around this time that I started to get more and more into the mind and how it worked.

Around that time, YouTube was just coming into my awareness and I was starting to watch videos and do my education about this stuff online.

You know when you go to YouTube

and you look at a video and then it shows you down the side of the screen eight other videos that might interest you, and then two that are completely unrelated to that video in any way. Before you know it, you're looking at cats falling off sofas and you're learning how to solve a Rubik's cube and stuff like that when you never had any interest in it before.

Then I saw down at the bottom of the screen when I was looking at a video, a hypnosis video. Just a video of somebody hypnotising somebody. I clicked on that because I had a vague interest in it before.

I started to follow this video paper trail through the world of hypnosis.

Then I chanced upon, funnily enough, one of your videos: Jon Chase talking about *frequently asked questions* in hypnosis.

As you will know very well, and anyone that's studied any hypnosis or even dipped their toe into it, will know there are as many different definitions of hypnosis as there are hypnotists. You get a different story about what it is from everyone.

I watched your video and I remember thinking, "I really hope that's what it is. Because if it is, I want to do that. I'd be interested in that."

I went onto your website. I saw that you had a weekend coming up in Swindon where you were going to teach hypnosis. I also saw that I'd just missed one in Croydon the weekend before, which is right down the road from me, so I was a bit gutted about that.

But instead I travelled to Swindon and I met you and we did a weekend workshop.

It blew my mind completely. It just opened up new possibilities to me.

I remember driving away from there on my hands-free talking to my partner at the time saying, "Oh my God. I've got magic powers." I couldn't believe what was going on.

It was a completely new world that had opened up to me. But I wasn't using it for anything therapeutic or to help people at all, because that wasn't my interest. I was just curious.

It was the same year I learned to juggle and I learned some magic tricks. It was just that sort of thing. Basically, I would just use it to impress people at the pub.

A friend of mine was a very good responder and was happy for me to hypnotise her.

We'd be in the pub. I'd stick her hand

to the table, get her to forget her name,
occasionally make her think the barmaid
had stolen her boobs, things like that.

Nothing I'm proud of, but-

Jon: I still do that.

Tim: This is it…when you're a young
hypnotist and you've just discovered
these magical powers!

But one day she said to me, "Why don't
you use this for something useful?"
I said, "I believe I am."
But then she said, "No no. Seriously.
I'm getting married, as you know, and I
don't want to wear false nails because
they're uncomfortable."

Yet, she was a massive nail biter. A real
chronic nail biter. She would bite her
nails when in front of the TV, of an
evening, and she would only notice she
was biting them when she started to

taste blood or she just felt that pain when she had gone a bit too far.

I said to her, "Look, I've not been trained in anything therapeutic. I don't know how to do this. It wouldn't be ethical. So let's have a go!"

We just had a go at it and I did it the same way a stage hypnotist would do it. I hypnotised her.

I said, "You don't bite your nails anymore. You remember you used to bite your nails, but you don't anymore. I'm not sure why, but you just don't do it." All that sort of thing. Woke her up, we looked at each other. Both said, "Well that didn't work, did it?" and got on with our lives.

Then, a couple of weeks later, she was round my house. We were watching TV or something, and she said, "By the way, I forgot to tell you, all my nails have grown back."

It was just this sudden shock that I experienced at that moment.

I would equate it to... you know you see in films or cartoons where the clouds part and the sun shines down and there's this aha-moment.

That's what it felt like to me.

I had to leave the room, because I was about to burst into tears.

I thought to myself when I did leave the room, I thought, "Oh, I'd like to feel that thing again. I'd love to feel that maybe every day." That's what led me down the road of: "I'm going to study this therapeutic and remedial side of hypnosis."

I got back in touch with you Jon; I did your therapeutic training.

I chased down other mentors, did all the diplomas, read all the books. I dived down the rabbit hole, basically, and it is a deep rabbit hole. Then I made this my career.

For the last seven years, I've been advancing and developing my techniques from working with clients full-time every day.

Most of them come with anxiety. That's what brings me here.

Interesting enough though, as an aside to that, I'm not a great hypnotic subject. I don't go, as you know, because you've been through this whole journey with me.

I remember the first weekend we were on, and by the Sunday afternoon you found me in a right hump because I couldn't get hypnotised the way other people were getting hypnotised.

I couldn't experience those things. You reminded me, "Look, you're not here to be hypnotised. You're here to hypnotise other people."

Ever since then I haven't really worried about it.

But, I've had things that I've needed to change about myself and I haven't had somebody hypnotise me and fix this for me.

I've had to develop ways of thinking about this to change my own mind.

When I first met you, that first morning, my social anxiety was at a real peak, because my hotel room was ... I could see where all of you guys were networking at the start of the day, having a coffee, getting to know each other.

Jon: I do. I do remember a very, very long-haired chap.

Tim: My protective curtain.

Jon: I thought hippy, scruffy, probably wears bells and he's going to call me "sensei."

It wasn't that at all. I do remember you sitting in the corner, and I did get a bit concerned on the second break that you weren't getting involved.

Tim: Absolutely. I was the guy that on the breakout session saying, "oh you practice, I'll just watch", because I couldn't engage.

When I arrived on that morning, deliberately after you'd all gone through and started to sit down, so that all that I needed to do was sit on my chair and experience the course without having to engage with people.

I remember you insisted, because you insist on shaking hands with everyone and saying "hello" to everyone, so it backfired on me because you called me to the front of the class where you were sitting and said, "Just say hello."

The first thing you said to me, because I had my protective curtain of fringe that I used to wear at that time...

Jon: Hiding behind the hair.

Tim: Hiding behind the hair. Exactly. You said to me, "Are you awake?" That's what you said to me.

I realise now it's because I looked such a state. But I thought at the time, "Is he doing something hypnosis-y with me? Is he getting into my mind or something like that?"

It freaked me out.

That weekend was massively challenging for me just to be there.

This is why I've had to find ways different to just hypnotising people and telling them to stop it, if you like.

Jon: Which works.

Tim: But it's not available to everyone, and also not what everyone wants.

When I'm working with my clients now, what we do is very eyes-open.

A lot of it is about understanding why your mind has created this effect for you so that you get the option to change it. I think with a lot of things that we treat, understanding is the key, but anxiety more than anything.

When we understand the purpose of it,

why it's happening, we can get rid of it very quickly.

What's going on?
A social anxiety
commentary

Jon: Okay, Tim. What do you think is going on currently in the world, in society, what's going on so as that anxiety sufferers need your anxiety control system even more than before?

Tim: When I started seeing clients for a living, I never had anyone come to me saying, "Can you help me with my anxiety?"

It wasn't a thing. People would come with issues that I would recognise were related to it, but it wasn't in the public awareness in the same way.

Now more than half the people I see are there to deal with anxiety. That's why

I run specific workshops on anxiety now, because help is so needed. It's so in-demand. I think I can only put it down to two things really.

First of all, because of the Internet we have access to a lot of information.

Certain things people are seeing are resonating with them, and the awareness that anxiety can be a thing that we have to deal with is now out there.

But also, the second thing is down to the Internet. There's more people on the planet than ever there has been.

We are now all connected to each other via this worldwide web.

We can click a button and communicate with somebody on the other side of the world who we've never even met.

We can insult them if we want to. We can point out something we don't like about them. As a result, we don't get any respite from this constant bombardment of information and interaction.

I was talking to an old schoolfriend the other day, and we were talking about, "Can you imagine if we'd had the Internet when we were at school and social media?"

As if it wasn't pressure enough when we were going through our schooldays at the time.

But at least we could go home and lift ourselves out of it for an evening and only have to go back to it when we went back to school.

People can't do that anymore.

They literally are connected to their

circle of friends and their circle of enemies at all times.

Oftentimes this doesn't stop when we leave school, when we grow up and we become adults. It just intensifies, because now we've got a bigger, wider circle of people that we can interact with.

I really put the fact that there's so much social anxiety now, down to our constant interaction online all the time.

We're not used to going out there and meeting people so much. As a result, we don't get any respite from the constant bombardment of that online interaction.

Jon: There's been some neurological research recently. Do you think people are losing their interpersonal skills?

Tim: Absolutely. There's neurological studies suggesting that the shape of people's brains is changing simply because different bits of it are growing than used to.

When we didn't have any sort of media...not just online, not just the web, but when we didn't have TVs and radios and all of our interaction was face to face, our brains would have been growing in a very different way.

We have 40 quadrillion active synaptic connexions in our brain that are constantly rewiring and reconfiguring according to what information we input via our senses.

It doesn't take a genius to work out that the way we input information into our brains these days is very different than it used to be.

We've got different challenges facing us in this day and age.

Jon: Do you see things staying pretty much

the way they are at least for the foreseeable future?

Tim: I don't see it getting any better for people. I don't see it getting any easier. Everything now is virtual.

You look at the biggest taxi firm in the world, Uber, they don't own any vehicles.

The biggest hoteliers, Airbnb, they don't own any property.

Everything is happening in cyberspace, including our relationships and our interactions with people.

There's always going to be now that inability, unless we literally turn off all our technology, we're not able to just take ourselves out of it so easily.

This is why you hear about people saying, "I'm deleting Facebook off of my phone, because I'm stuck with it. I'm constantly scrolling and looking at it, and it's just rubbish that isn't making me feel anything but bad." This is why people are doing that.

It's probably only going to get more intense.

There's going to be that point where we take pictures by blinking our eyes and then we send them to somebody by thinking about them! It's not going to be too far away.

We're going to have to learn to manage ourselves better, because the world isn't going to change for us. It isn't going to settle down for us at all.

Jon: Do you see that as a specific area for anxiety sufferers, where you see things are going to get ... Are things going to get shaken up and they're going to have a major impact? What's going to shape the future?

Tim: I think hopefully...rather than predicting doom and disaster, I tend to look towards how we're managing it and how we're responding to it.

When we originally met, we would talk like there's no way we're going to get any sort of mindfulness or understanding of your subconscious into schools. It just isn't going to happen. People didn't want their kids being subjected to anyone with hypnosis training or the understanding of all this stuff.

These days, mindfulness is in schools. There is a great desire to bring in people that can teach our kids emotional intelligence.

That makes perfect sense to me, because we teach kids all these sorts of things that they maybe will never use, like history, and we're giving them all the life skills and the practical skills in terms of English literature, English language, maths, all the stuff they're going to hopefully be using when they're out in the business world and they're out conducting their lives.

But we haven't thus far been giving them any education on how to manage their emotions.

I think that the big innovation and revolution in terms of education, is going to be when we start to teach people how to protect themselves from this constant bombardment of potentially negative information and input.

Anxiety and the purpose of emotions

Jon: Let's get down to basics. What is
        anxiety?

Tim: Anxiety, when you break it down to its
        most basic level, is an emotion.

        I know that sounds like the most
        ridiculously obvious thing to say at the
        start of this, but I think a lot of people
        that are reading this book or listening to
        this broadcast, they have a different
        framework for anxiety.

        They regard it as a condition, a disorder,
        or even an illness. They think this for a
        very good reason: because somebody in
        a position of medical authority has told
        them that that's exactly what this is.

        But anxiety, I'm going to encourage you

people that are reading this to think about anxiety slightly differently now.

It's an emotion. Nothing more than that. An emotion that we can either lose control of or get control of. If we can do that, then we can start to view things a little bit differently.

Basically, if you're going to understand what anxiety is doing on an emotional level, you have to understand what emotions are for.

To understand what emotions are for, you have to understand how your mind works, or certainly the model of the mind that I'm talking about when I'm educating people.

Jon: Could you explain the purpose of emotions? Why do we have emotions?

Tim: That's a really broad-reaching question. Your emotions are the tools of your subconscious.

If we break the mind down to two sections, conscious and subconscious. (I feel like I'm telling this to somebody who told it to me originally, so this is really interesting).

Your **conscious** is your logical, rational, reasoning part of your thinking.

It's your point of immediate focus, the bit that hopefully some people are still paying attention to me with at the moment.

It's capable of doing maybe a handful of things at once, at most, with any degree of competence.

Anything more than that, we've got to get rid of something out of our conscious awareness to put something else in there. It has a limited capacity.

By contrast, your **subconscious** is constantly doing hundreds and hundreds and hundreds of things all in the background, and most of it outside of our conscious awareness.

It's our emotional, imaginative, and creative part of our thinking.

Most importantly, for someone like me, it's the bit that holds all of our belief systems and our thoughts and behavioural patterns.

Anything you feel you do without thinking, can't stop doing, or can't start doing, that's because there's an automatic pattern of thought running in your subconscious that is driving that behaviour.

If we're going to look to change something about what's happening automatically, we've got to get access to that pattern of thought in some way.

Up to the age of about eight or nine, we were almost purely subconscious in the way we were processing things.

We were emotional, in the moment.

We saw it, we did it, we learnt, and we sponged up in those early years all of that information and formed what I sometimes refer to as our 'map of reality.' Our idea about how the world works.

Then, around that age, about eight or nine, we started to develop our more logical, conscious way of thinking.

What came with our conscious mind is this thing that hypnotists, like you and I, would refer to as the 'critical faculty.' That was an Elman thing, wasn't it? He came up with that.

Whatever you want to call it, however you want to refer to it, the job of this bit of your thinking is to protect your reality.

Basically, when new information comes in, it judges it for truth. It acts like a security guard around your subconscious.

That's what I'm going to refer to it as from now is, the '*security guard.*'

If something new comes in, if it doesn't match up with or isn't at least compatible with what's on your map of reality, that *security guard* will just reject it as false, no matter how logical it seems to your conscious thinking.

The example we always use, let's say four or five years old, a spider runs out in the kitchen. *Mum* screams, jumps on a chair, (apologies for suggesting people's life is like a Tom and Jerry cartoon), our learning mind says, "Okay. That's the appropriate response to those things because *Mum* just did it and that's who we're learning from."

Jon: Can I stop you there? Can we get politically correct here and say that men do that as well, by the way.

Tim: They do. Oh God yes! They absolutely do. In fact, I see more men for spider phobia than I do for the women.

But anyway, this information goes into our mind, onto our map of reality, and every spider we see for the rest of our lives, our heart beats faster, we tense up, we sweat, we get that fear response. Even though logically we're thinking, "That's tiny. That can't possibly hurt me. I should just be able to pick that up and put it outside." But the reason we can't is because all that logical information is being rejected by that security guard because it doesn't match up with what we already know: Spiders are scary.

It's our problem that stops us solving the problem.

What we've got to do, really, we've got to do something that gets us past that security guard.

We talk about inducing a state of what we would call "subconscious dominance," where instead of trying to get past that security guard and get in the building, we just take everything that's of interest to us in that building, put it out here where I am, and speak directly to it. We use your imagination, we use your emotions, we use the things that your subconscious does really, really well on its own to achieve that.

But, if you break this down in terms of what's actually happening, I tend to think of the mind like a ship, if you can bear with me for this analogy, and that ship has a captain and a crew.

In this analogy, the **captain** is your **logical, conscious, rational mind.** It knows where we're going, knows why we're going there. It's got an idea of how we're going to get there, as well. It has a plan.

Unfortunately, the bit of us that has all its hands on the things that steer and sail the ship is the **subconscious.** That's the **crew**, basically.

If your **crew** is listening to your **captain**, it's plain sailing.

You have an idea, you know where you want to go in life, and then all of your subconscious crewmen, they do the things they need to do to get us there, and we feel in control of the ship.

We only really feel out of control of the

ship when our crew aren't listening to the captain and they're doing their own thing, they're all everywhere.

The reason this happens, the reason we have our crew members just doing things they want to do rather than what we want them to do, is because all the jobs that they're assigned on the ship were assigned before we had a captain on board, before we had a logical, conscious adult rational mind operating for us.

All the motivation for that crew in those early years was "Learn what we can as fast as we can. Keep the ship afloat." All of these jobs that your crew are doing, all of these patterns of thought are stuck in there, and they might not be relevant now.

They might not be appropriate to how you want to live your life and where you want to sail your ship.

But what we've got to do is to get access to them and introduce new jobs.

To come back originally to what we were talking about here in terms of the purpose of emotions, emotions are the puppet strings by which your subconscious moves you around.

For example, if we were to regard something as dangerous, like that spider we were talking about, a crew member onboard your ship says, "Right. We'll trigger the appropriate emotion to keep us away from the dangerous thing: Fear."

You feel afraid. Whatever that is, a churning in the stomach, tightness in the chest, whatever it might be.

The only way of getting comfortable again is to move away from the dangerous thing. Your crew achieves what it's trying to do and sails the ship where it needs to go.

Let's say it's anger. Anger is, "I have been wronged. I now need to right the wrong." You adrenalize.

There's that bit of you that says, "I will not let you rest until you say something to that person or you do something to right this wrong," and you've got anger going on.

It's going to try and motivate you to go and punch that person or say something to them or tell them off or something like that.

Anxiety is no different. It is an emotion that your subconscious mind triggers in order to basically find the best strategy for the most happiness.

Anxiety is, "There's something

important in my mind that must come into my conscious attention."

If it's really big, then it has to stay there. It is, "I've got a test coming up. I need to revise for it." "I'm going to drive to this place tomorrow. I'm not sure the direction I'm going in."

It's that stuff that says, "This is important. Pay attention to it."

Jon: "Tomorrow I'm going to speak to 2,000 people."

Tim: Exactly. It's a big thing. Before, you're feeling the anxiety, anticipating it.

But this is the thing. We sometimes get the idea that those crewmen are fighting against us by giving us this horrible feeling that feels like an illness.

It feels terrible. But really, every single crew member is hardwired to try and find the best strategy for the most happiness.

Happiness is our motivation.

You will sometimes get told, "No. It's safety. It's keeping us alive that's the motivation."

We can understand that. But if that was the only motivation, keeping us safe, keeping us alive, you wouldn't see people leaping out of a plane just for the lols, or jumping off of a bridge with bungee straps attached to them just for the thrill of it.

You certainly wouldn't see people ending their lives because they have a shortage of happiness.

Safety is a big component part of happiness, but it's not the be all and end all of our motivation.

If we can communicate, as we were talking about, in the right way with our subconscious, we can deliver new information to get it to do better things for us. That's the purpose of emotion, is to get us to where we need to be. We've just got to help those members of our crew by guiding them a little bit better.

What causes anxiety to get out of hand?

Jon: We just heard that anxiety is a marker for important stuff.

Tim: It's exactly that.

Jon: I thought you would, because I know that you actually say that in your notes for your workshops and stuff. I thought I'd bring that up.

Tim: I think you're right.

Jon: That's wonderfully clear. Thank you. What causes anxiety? I know we were touching on it, but can we get just a little bit more detail here?

What causes, in a very logical, very understandable way, what causes anxiety to get out of hand?

Tim: The way it tends to start, certainly in my
        experience personally, and working with
        people with this, is that something big
        comes into your life that you've got to
        take care of. It might be health. It might
        be a situation at work. It could be, like
        you say, you've got to speak to people
        for something coming up. It just sits
        there not having anything done to it.

        An example would be I saw a client
        once who had a trial coming up for
        something they didn't do in six months
        time. They were feeling tremendous
        constant levels of anxiety about the
        upcoming trial, but they didn't want to
        be existing with this horrible feeling in
        their chest for six months.

        All their mind is doing there is saying,
        "This is really, really important. It might
        be the most important thing in our life
        for the next few years. So we can't just

forget about it. We can't just throw it away and ignore it, because it's too important."

What happens then is that crew member whose job it is to look after this activity starts to shout louder and louder because nothing's really being done.

We're just sitting there getting on with our lives without addressing it directly.

But six months out, he'd done everything he needed to do. He prepped everything. He got his brief.

He didn't really have to think about this until a day or two before the actual trial when he would need to get his head in the game.

But you've still got this crew member saying, "No no. This is the most important thing in our lives, and I'm going to keep shouting about it."

Then what happens is you've got all these other crew members on the ship who have fairly mundane things to do, like remember to get the shopping, remember to put the bins out, stuff like that. But then, to actually get heard, they have to shout even louder than the bit that's really shouting. Otherwise, it will get ignored and it will just get forgotten.

What you've got now is a whole load of **crew** members **shouting** really, *really* **loudly** at the captain of the ship, at your *conscious mind*, into your *conscious awareness*. Before you know it you've got no idea what you're anxious about, because it's just a ship full of people **shouting** at you.

Then, as a result of this, you might get told, "You have anxiety."

Your anxiety has now escalated and

now you have chemicals in your brain being created that are causing you to constantly have anxiety, and now you've got a... disorder.

Then suddenly you've got someone else shouting in there about your health, about your mental health and the worries that you have.

"Will this anxiety ever leave?" Because sometimes what happens is we'll get to the other side of that important thing and we'll *still* have those high levels of anxiety because everyone's got used to shouting now and no one's going to just decide to whisper when everyone else in the room is shouting.

They just keep doing it at this level.

Basically, what becomes the biggest thing you're anxious about is this constant level of anxiety, even though the big thing you were anxious about previously has now passed.

I had a client actually that did exactly this. She came to see me.

She'd been diagnosed with health anxiety and generalised anxiety. She was told she had a disorder. She'd been put on medication to treat it. She's had a course of CBT.

She saw me as a last resort, which I'm okay about. I don't seem to be many people's *first* choice. They don't say, "There's something wrong. I'm going to go and see the hypnotist."

They tend to go to the doctor first, which is fair enough.

But it had started a couple years earlier, and it was a really good time in her life. She was doing brilliantly. In fact, her business was flying and she was winning awards and she was getting big contracts doing better than she could ever have imagined. But as a result she was working quite hard, doing quite long hours.

She was out with her friends one day in town and, for whatever reason, she hadn't had much sleep, she hadn't eaten very well, she hadn't taken enough fluids, so physically she was a bit run down.

She started to feel ill. She started to feel her heart beating a bit faster, breathing getting a bit erratic, feeling a bit dizzy, and she started to really worry about what this was.

Before she knew it, she'd amplified it and talked herself into a panic attack.

The ambulance was called. Panic attacks feel like you're dying, don't they? So she had a really big scare health-wise.

What then happened was she went to the doctor. The doctor said it's anxiety, and she started to worry about her anxiety.

The biggest thing in her life that she was worrying about was that now she'd made herself ill and she now had anxiety, that she would just have to manage for the rest of her life.

The first thing you've got to do in those situations is understand the anxiety comes and goes. It's normal, but if we manage it correctly it shouldn't be any higher than anyone else's anxiety.

I think the danger here is that we believe when we're told we have something, we will always have it.

We've talked about change already. Change is inevitable. Our brain grows every day. We're constantly inputting information. We'll never get stuck with something going on up here that isn't changeable. As a result, we do have the option to take control of how we grow our brain from day to day.

We have this thing now, because we've got Facebook, we do this thing where it shows your picture you put up a year ago.

It says, "A year ago you were here doing this."

You look at the picture and you think, "Really? That was just a year ago? That seems like ages longer than that. I'm completely different than I was when I was there. I remember what I was thinking. I remember what I was saying to people. I'm nothing like that now."

Yet, we imagine that we've just been the same person from that day to this day.

But every day we grow and evolve and

improve hopefully, just by little increments.

Then when we see the difference we realise, "Actually I'm changing all the time." All we've really got to do is say, "I'm going to play an active part in deciding how I change from day to day, rather than allowing life to decide how I change."

What can we do about it?

Jon: You've already mentioned this, that people such as you are not, generally speaking, people's first choice.

Although, whether that's a lack of education, that hopefully Hypnoarts books like this can change.

But what can we actually do about it? What do people tend to do first? What about doctors?

Tim: Yeah, it's doctors. Because anxiety feels so physical, it is such a ... well it manifests in your body.

I hear people all the time saying it's a gripping of the chest. It just feels like something's got a hold of you. It can be your heart beating faster. It can be feeling constantly adrenalized and in a state of panic when it really gets bad. So, we go to the doctor.

I love doctors. They've saved me more than once. I'm a big fan of doctors. But I'm not a fan of going to see a doctor for a mental health issue, because doctors are not the experts in that field.

If you want a doctor who is a mental health expert, you see a psychiatrist, who do four or five more years of training on top of their normal medical training, and then they know a little bit more about what's going on up here.

Doctors get between 8 and 10 minutes with us to diagnose what it might be that's going on. Their job is to find out if this is something physical, something medical, that they can test for and they can then treat with medication.

When we have something medical going

on, we go to the doctor. We say, "Here are my symptoms."

They say, "Hm. It sounds like this thing. Let's send you for tests to check whether it is or not."

The tests come back. Maybe they're positive. They say, "Right. I thought it was. Let me give you this treatment."

They know what it is. They've got the treatment for it.

With mental health stuff like anxiety or depression they will do the tests, but the tests are simply to rule out the possible *physical* causes of these symptoms. When they've ruled them out they will say, "Right. You have anxiety."

The trouble is they can't test for anxiety. They can't say, "Let me run this scan and I'll find out what sort of anxiety you have." All they have is the report of the person telling them what's going on...

their symptoms, basically.

Then they medicate for the symptoms.

People are given medication now for anxiety.

The only other option is to go and refer them to a counsellor, which is generally a cognitive behavioural therapist.

CBT is what you get, certainly in this country on the NHS, that's what they go for. But the problem with this is there is a standard waiting time of about 12 weeks.

I've had someone come to see me and say, "Well, I went to see the doctor last week. They've prescribed *emergency* CBT for me."
I said, "Right. Okay. So when are you seeing them?"
He said, "Well, in about four weeks I'll get a letter telling me when the

appointment is, and that might be four to eight weeks in the future." It just didn't sound tremendously emergency to me. It was a long wait.

If you're a doctor, and you've got someone in front of you in absolute dire straits, literally in anguish with what's going on with them physically and emotionally, and you say to them, "Right. In 12 weeks time you'll go and see someone that might be able to tell you what's going on."

That's not much help. All they've got really are medication. It's meds. It's pills.

But that comes with other problems, which I'm not going to go into, because I don't deal with medication.

I'm not a psychiatrist. I'm not a doctor. But I know that when somebody comes with anxiety, I know I can probably offer them a better understanding than a doctor could, and not just because they'll get longer with me than 8 to 10 minutes, if you know what I mean.

Doctors are not the best course of action.

The other reason why they're not your best option is because what they will do is, they will label you.

Again, I'm **not blaming doctors** for this, because what happens when you see a doctor, if you come back for another appointment you might get the same doctor.

You might have a completely different doctor.

They have to put a name on what they're seeing you about so that the next doctor that reads your notes can go, "Okay. It's this we're dealing with."

They have to give you that label. But what they tend to do is, you go into the doctor's with a symptom and they give you a load of baggage because they said, "Right. You have an anxiety disorder."

Now you're that person with the anxiety disorder.

For an anxious person, to know they now have a disorder, where the inference is you're always going to have it, that's a tremendous source of anxiety. It doesn't help in any way.

Currently the way we're treating this is not the most helpful.

Jon: Would you say that modern diagnosis makes it worse?

Tim: I think. I might whisper that. I wouldn't shout it.

Jon: Whisper that very loudly.

Tim: I don't want to offend the doctor who might be treating someone in there. But, yeah, basically. It just adds to our pain. It adds to the things we're dealing with.

Anxiety is…it's overwhelm. It's too much going on up there. "Let's give you another thing to worry about." It doesn't help at all.

When I see people, the first thing I'm looking to do is make sure they understand this kind of life sentence they've been given was inaccurate.

Most of the time, and I mean most of the time like 90+% of the time, anxiety is got under control very, very easily and very, very quickly. Because if we talk to the right bit of you that's doing this and we give it an option to do something better, it won't hang around doing the rubbish thing. It'll go for the good thing.

What are the alternatives?

Jon: What are the alternatives to the established medical approaches?

Tim: The alternatives? There are loads of alternative treatments for anxiety.

You could do something that's more 'relax-o-therapy' based, because I know a lot of people get a lot of benefit from just having an hour to themselves, having a massage, having some sort of alternative therapy done with them so they can just basically release some of that tension that they feel physically.

But really, the best way of treating anxiety is with information.

It's *understanding* that opens the door to get us out of this prison that we're in.

I remember somebody contacted me from America. It was a lady who was really worried about her daughter who was constantly catastrophizing.

I think she was only ... she was only young. Something like 11 or 12, or maybe even younger than that.

No, that's right. She was eight or nine I think. She would, if she saw a knife in…

Jon: I'm going to stop you there. Constantly catastrophizing?

Tim: Yeah.

Jon: "Catastrophe" with "-izing" on the end?

Tim: That's pretty much what it is, yeah.

Jon: Okay. I like that.

Tim: Are we going to look that word up at

the end of this and see if it's real?

Jon: Yeah. We've got a transcription coming up.

Tim: Okay. That one's going to have a big red line underneath it.

Jon: Yeah. Check spelling on this. {*Note from publisher. We did look it up, it's not a word but we like it. So it's in. JB*}

Tim: Okay. She was constantly predicting disaster. She would see a knife in a room and then she wouldn't be able to stop thinking about, "Don't cut yourself on the knife."

         Any potential hazard or trip hazard, anything like that, she would constantly be really, really worried about it.

         Her mum didn't really know what to do about it, so she asked my advice.

         I basically told her about the captain

and the crew, and let her sort of explain that there's a bit of you trying to look after you, but it's just doing it slightly too enthusiastically, if you see what I mean.

That bit of you is a real friend to you but it's a friend that you need to get to calm down a bit.

She came back to me and she sent me these pictures of these drawings they'd done.

Her mum had sat her down and she'd said to her daughter, "If you had a company that you were running what would it be?"

This little girl said, "Well, it would be Disneyland." She drew a picture of her at the desk at Disneyland. She then started to draw all the staff that she had at Disneyland and she gave them names and she drew pictures of them.

One of them was Karen, and Karen is in charge of security. Karen comes up to the front desk and tells her when there's, "Oh, there's a danger there. There's a danger there." But the problem is, and this was her words, "Karen gets crazy sometimes," and Karen just stays there saying it over and over again, when really she needs to just let us know and then go away and go and do her job again.

So she created Roger, and Roger's job is when Karen gets crazy, to walk her away from the desk and tell her to get on with her job.

This understanding that she now has completely sorts out the excessive anxiety, because she *understands* now that her mind's trying to work for her. If she works with it, there's no problem. I think the alternative is the understanding.

You'll notice what we've covered in there as well is, **being kind to yourself.**

Not beating yourself up.

Not treating that bit of you like the enemy.

It's actually a really, really good friend.

I think that, generally speaking, is how we need to deal with anxiety as a whole, not just this country but in other countries as well. **We have to get the understanding.**

If we understand what our emotions are for and why they're happening, we can achieve greater control over them.

Jon: When does your mind stop shouting?

Tim: Your mind stops shouting when it knows it doesn't have to shout.

I'll do work and I'll talk to people's

subconscious. Us hypnotists, we talk directly to the subconscious.

I remember you telling me this. This is me preaching to the choir here, I know. But we're never talking to the conscious. **We're talking to the crew at all times.**

If we open up new options, then ... If we tell that crew that's just all shouting, that, "Nobody needs to shout, and if **you all shout nobody gets heard.** Nobody gets understood and nothing gets done."

We basically ask the crew to start doing what we actually *should* be doing with anxiety, which is *whispering* or *nudging* or just pointing out things.

When everyone is silent, as a rule, without anything going on, we're just silent, then every whisper gets heard.

This is why when we're in a library we can hear everyone's whispered conversation across the other table or across the room, because there's no other sound.

When we're at, I don't know, the Stock Exchange or we're in the pub and everyone's talking really, really loudly, we're lucky if we can hear the person who's actually talking straight to us trying to tell us something.

We don't hear everyone's conversation in a shouting room because there's too much noise going on and our mind is kind of doing this. "I just want to come away from all this noise!"

Jon: Your mind's constantly putting its fingers in its ears.

Tim: Kind of, yeah. Any message that you want to deliver then is not getting heard because there's too much shouting going on.

Calming the mind is about just encouraging your subconscious to whisper things.

That's really about, as I say, understanding the motivation behind the shouting so that you can allow that bit to feel at ease.

It's like when somebody's in a panic and they're banging on the door, there's an emergency.

If we just ignore it and just hope it will go away, but they know we're in here, they're just going to keep banging louder until we answer the door.

If we answer the door and say, "Okay. I understand." Turns out, you don't need to worry about it. It's not an emergency. You thought it was, but it isn't.

If we can actually relate directly to that part, it can calm down, it can go away, and it can stop banging on the bloody door!

What does your mind need to know?

Jon: In the notes for this interview you gave me 10 steps, 10 points that you wanted to cover. If for getting your mind to whisper, clearing you mind is the answer, what do anxiety sufferers need to know about these 10 major things?

Tim: I've broken it down to 10 things. There are probably more than these, but in my mind, to my thinking, if your subconscious understands these 10 things at a belief level, then you shouldn't be troubled with excessive or high levels of anxiety again.

1. Worrying is never the best strategy

Tim: The first thing is to understand that worrying is never the best strategy.

I have a very specific definition for worrying.

We do puzzle solving and we do pondering and thinking about things all the time, but normally we ponder about something, we think about it, we solve a puzzle, and we take action.

When we're pondering things that we can't take action on, that's when it's called worrying.

If you find yourself doing the thing you would call worrying, you know you've got a crew member in there doing the wrong thing, wasting its time and wasting its energy. Your mind doesn't like to do that, so you've got to direct it to do something else.

I had a client come in and her worrying seemed perfectly legitimate and perfectly valid.

Her son had just turned 18. The first night he'd gone out with his mates on his own he got beaten up. He got in a fight and it had been a terrible time. She had to go to A&E to meet him and all that sort of thing.

Then every time he went out, panic. She couldn't rest. As a mother, she was constantly pacing.

She's that mum that was texting him all the time, "Are you okay?" If he didn't text straight back she'd really get panicky and really worried.

She'd be awake until he got in. She was exhausting herself and just destroying her mind and her health with worry about him.

You might think, "Well, that's understandable. He got beaten up."

But what we had to tell her subconscious was that, all the time he's out you have no idea what he's doing, and all this worrying is just exhausting and damaging you.

I said, "Let's imagine that you did get a call. 'Mum, I'm in A&E again.' Or, 'I need you to pick me up.' An exhausted, fraught, frantic version of you isn't the best to take action to help him.

The best version of you is a rested, relaxed, calm version of you that just says, "Okay. I'll come and do that." You've got to be at your best if that's the case.

But the other thing we told that lady's subconscious, that crew member, was that he was an adult now, and that crew member was operating as if he was still that kid that it's her duty to look after.

It comes to that point where you say, "You know what? It's your job to look after you. It's my job to look after me."

If we class ourselves doing something that's what we would call worrying, that is when we need to change what we do.

2. Make your mind a library

Jon: Number two.

Tim: Second thing. It comes back to what we were just talking about.

Make your mind a library. Make sure that everyone in there is whispering or at least talking at a low level rather than shouting at you.

The way we do this, once we've got a better control and the shouting has died down, we just basically listen to it.

We listen to what your anxiety is about.

The curse of the person that is suffering high levels of anxiety is that they can't hear the detail.

When I have people coming back to me say for a followup appointment who have now got control of their anxiety, the thing they tell me probably most often is, "The interesting thing is now if I feel anxiety I know what it's about. I know what I'm feeling anxious about now, whereas I didn't before. It was just this huge feeling in me."

All the time that we listen and we take action on the things that we might feel anxious about we get stuff done and we don't let the anxiety get out of control anymore.

A lot of that is about recognising whether you're being spoken to by a crew member that is doing the right thing or the wrong thing in terms of, "Am I feeling anxious about something I can take action on or something I can do nothing about? Is it my stuff or somebody else's stuff I'm feeling anxious about?"

The ability to let that bit know, "You can stand down. You can have a rest. You don't have to be getting into my face and telling me all about this stuff now."

3. Panic is redundant

Jon: Great. Number three.

Tim: Number three is just this idea that
        panic, as in the 10 out of 10 anxiety
        level that we feel, is no longer
        applicable.

        This is a response we have from the
        days when we had to hunt and kill
        things to stay alive and we had to kill
        other people to stop them killing us.

        Panic is that fight-or-flight thing we
        maybe need once or twice in our lives if
        we're unlucky.

        It's not something that we generally
        need anymore. If your subconscious has
        got the idea that at any time levels of
        five, six, seven, eight, or nine out of 10
        on the anxiety scale is appropriate, then
        it's got the wrong idea.

I spoke to a client once and we do these things sometimes where we get their subconscious talking through them, if that makes sense to the people reading this. (I know it will make sense to you, Jon).

When we get this thing we call ideo-motor response, where your subconscious takes over and just talks to us.

I had a lady doing this and I was talking to her subconscious and I was saying, "You know what? It's really only appropriate now for things like car crashes or bear attacks."
She added, "Tsunamis." She just blurted it out.
I was like, "Yeah. Maybe tsunamis, actually. That's something as well."

But the point being that it's never really necessary in our everyday life, where the biggest thing we feel anxious about is getting to that meeting tomorrow, getting that report in, or, as I said before, taking the bins out.

We only need the whispers, the one or two out of 10. Knowing that panic is not something we will generally need much in our lives these days is of value as well.

4. Anxiety is not your name

Jon: Number four.

Tim: Number four on the hit parade.

Jon: Number four. I'm getting you to the 10.

Tim: I know. **Anxiety is not your name.**

That's how I say it to people. But we sometimes make the mistake of thinking that we *are* anxiety.

"This is who I am. This is a part of me, and if I got rid of it I wouldn't be me anymore."

I think what I'm always trying to let people know when they come in to see me, because they're wearing this label that they've been given, and they might be known in their social circle as the person who feels that high anxiety, who *might* be able to come out at the weekend but probably won't because their anxiety will stop them coming out.

Then, when you identify with that person and you think, "This is who I am," then suddenly you don't have the option of being anything else because it would radically change who you are.

It's the difference between doing a certain job, let's say our job is to be a janitor, and then saying that, "Once that job is done, I don't exist anymore." This is not who you are. It's just what you're doing at the moment.

That crew member that's in there that says, "I'm the bit that's triggering the anxiety for you,"
if it thinks that to stop triggering anxiety it would have nothing to do anymore, it wouldn't exist anymore, then it might actually resist stopping doing it. It might actually think,
"For me to have any purpose in this

world I have to be that high level of anxiety."

We've just got to let that bit know that, "Actually, you can do whatever you want."

No one wants to be that guy pointing at everything that's going wrong and pointing at everything that's bad about potentially what's going to happen in their lives.

We want that part of your subconscious, that crew member, to say, "You know what? I'll do something better. I'll do something more positive, something more enjoyable." The person will feel the effects of that as well.

5. The feeling is natural

Jon: Number five. Is it natural?

Tim: Yes. This feeling is natural.

You need to know that you'll always
feel anxiety. It's not because it's going
to be a bad thing. It's because it's one
of your emotions.

If you didn't feel anxiety, you would be
one emotion short of a full set.

Then you really *would* have a disorder!

You need to know that when you get all
those levels down the trouble we have
then is sometimes people will hear that
whisper of anxiety going on, they'll
awake in the morning and have
something going on in the day that
they're feeling a bit anxious about, and
then before you know it they're starting
to think, "Oh my god, my anxiety's

coming back!"

It's not.

We will never have completely zero anxiety every moment of our lives, because then we wouldn't care about anything. We wouldn't be preparing for things. We wouldn't make sure we were in a position in our lives where we needed to be.

Anxiety is important. *It is a friend,* because it gives you good advice.

It points your attention to places where it needs to be. When it's at the appropriate level, it's really handy.

But we shouldn't ever be trying to say, "This is an unnatural feeling. This is a disorder."

Anxiety is an emotion.

As a result, we utilise all the emotions

that our mind throws us to get us where we need to be. It's a natural feeling. It's not unnatural.

6. The way it feels differs from the way it is

Jon: Number six.

Tim: The mistake we commonly make is that *the way it feels is the way it is.*

This happens when people start to regard their anxiety as an enemy or a part of them that's there to make them miserable or curse them or beat them up. It feels like that.

I absolutely recognise it feels like that. Even though I can't say ... some people that come to me with anxiety... I can't say I've ever had the levels of anxiety they're experiencing.

It would be easy for them to say, "Well, you don't know what this exactly feels like, so you don't know how it is."

But it's for that very reason that I can

help, because I'm not down there in the pit with you. I'm outside the pit pulling you up.

If I believe that the way it feels to you is the way it is, I wouldn't be able to help you, because the way you think it is at the moment, you can't help yourself because of that framework.

It's my job to say, "You know what? I know it feels like this, but it is different."

That's the mistake that oftentimes anxiety sufferers or depression sufferers fall into. It's a trap to think, "Because you don't know how I'm feeling you can't help me." When actually it's because we know how the mind works that we can help you.

Don't buy into the reality that your mind has given you, because you've already recognised that's not the best version of reality out there.

7. The folly of Jürgen Klopp

Jon: Number seven.

Tim: We've touched on this already, the idea
        of not beating yourself up.

        I always use this example. It was last
        year 2016. I know some of you are
        going to be football fans and some of
        you are not going to be football fans.

        Understanding football is not necessary
        to understand this analogy.

        I saw a game where we had Liverpool
        and Southampton, two teams in the
        English Premier League.

        Liverpool were winning this game by a
        long way. They were all over
        Southampton. They had all the
        possession. They were smashing it.

        They were two-nill up at halftime,

which for anyone that knows football, you think, "Right. I've got the game won there."

After the break the second half started and Southampton got a goal back, so it was two-one.

Then, straight after that, the Liverpool centre forward, was clear on goal, and pretty much you go three-one up halfway through the second half, it's sorted. It's game over.

But he missed, he missed quite badly.

Then, subsequently, Southampton went on to score two more goals and win the game three-two.

The Liverpool manager, Jürgen Klopp, as the whistle went, came tearing off the touchline screaming his head off at the centre forward who had missed the open goal earlier on in the game. He got right up in his face.

The cameras saw him absolutely tearing seven shades off of him.

They went back to the studio where, Gary Lineker, Alan Shearer, do their analysis.

Alan Shearer said, "I think he might regret that. Because in the midst of all of that, in front of the cameras, in front of the players, in front of the fans, he's had a go at him.

Jürgen Klopp at some point in the near future is going to want that forward to do something amazing for him, to go the extra mile, to be the superstar.

He might be less inclined to go the extra mile for the person that hung him out to dry in front of the fans."

If Jürgen Klopp had run off the touchline, and instead of screaming at him had put his arm around him and said, "You know what? Everyone misses. I bet you get the next one, and we'll be there cheering you on when you do."

If he'd have walked him down the touchline as all the fans around the tunnel were screaming and spitting at him and all that sort of thing and was his protection during that, then maybe he would get a better response from that player in the future.

Subsequently, that player left the club at the end of the season.

Whenever he's now on the pitch with Liverpool players, he's trying to score *against* them.

The lesson here that I took from that is how many times do we beat ourselves up when we do something bad, or we don't perform in the way we wanted to, or we mess up in some way?

How many times do we chastise ourselves about it? If all you're going to do is beat yourself up, all you're going to end up is beaten.

Whenever you're dealing with this stuff, you've got to make sure you're treating yourself with *kindness*, because that crew member that you're shouting at effectively by beating yourself up is doing its best; because we only generally shout at people when we don't think they're trying hard enough or they know what they should be doing, but for some reason they're not doing it.

Instead they're shouting at them, thinking maybe that would give them a kick up the ass and get them going.

But if all you're looking to do is educate them, this part thinks its doing the right thing, and it's doing its best within the framework of that right thing.

If you're looking to educate rather than castigate, then just deliver the message with kindness.

Because, as we've already said, you shout at somebody, they do this; They put their fingers in their ears. That doesn't help them at all. That doesn't help you change the way your mind is thinking.

We say this a lot, "Oh, be kind to yourself." But there's a deeper reason for that than I think we understand in our everyday life.

You are shouting at a member of your crew who you can't throw overboard, you can't change, you can't substitute. They're always going to be there and they're always going to be doing some sort of job for you. How do you think you're going to get the best out of them?

8. The cognitive assessment

Jon: Number eight.

Tim: Number eight. This comes back to one of the most important things we can do, which is make sure we get our rest and our sleep.

We do this thing whenever a challenge comes in; we call it a cognitive assessment, where our mind says, "Do I have the resources to deal with this challenge?" If we don't, we start to feel anxiety.

There's a couple of reasons for this.

It could be that crew member is trying to steer us away from it and shut down and get lost.

It could be we do a call for help; we could collapse on the floor and burst into tears and hope that somebody comes and saves us like they did when we were a kid. Or we could do that adrenalizing thing, where we draw all the resources from our body and our mind in a fight-or-flight panic response to try and deal with this challenge.

But what happens is that if we haven't had our rest, (just exactly like that lady I was talking about when she was out with her friends in town when she hadn't had enough sleep), we leave ourselves vulnerable to the more extreme responses to deal with challenges.

We always have to remember that if we don't look after ourselves then we're going to be low on resources.

Our subconscious will recognise the difficulty we're about to have with something, and we might go into some sort of panic or anxiety state.

If we get our rest; if we wake in the morning feeling absolutely brilliant, then the day is a very different day. The world is a different place. The things that look like mountains before are just little bumps, and we smash everything. We do it great.

The problem here is that when we feel anxious it stops us sleeping, because we're concerned with things and our mind is focusing on things that we should be leaving alone.

Then when we lose our sleep we're prone to more anxiety because we're low on resources; so it feeds into itself.

We always have to be mindful of getting our rest and making sure that we're not leaving ourselves vulnerable to this stuff.

Always be aware of this stuff.

9. You are the expert on you

Jon: Number nine.

Tim: When we were talking about social
         media and the pressures it puts on you,
         a lot of those pressures come from the
         fear of judgement; your social circle and
         the way we could be ostracised from it.

         I'm going to tell you a story.

         About a year ago I got an electrician in
         my building to fix the fire alarms.

         He came in and I said, "Right, what you
         need to do, I think you need to run the
         wires from here. If you go along here, I
         think you need a fuse. It's this size in
         the fuse box for that."

         He's looking at me like I'm mad or
         something. I said, "Shall I just let you
         do it?"

He said, "Yeah. Go on."

Because the thing is, I know nothing about electrics; I was trying to tell him how to do the job he was the expert on.

At the same time, if he'd burst into my session with my client and told me how to run a hypnosis session, I probably wouldn't have listened to him, because I'm the expert on that and he's not.

The point being, there is one subject that every single person in the world is the world's leading expert on.

That is ourselves.

What we tend to do, we tend to modify ourselves to please the opinion that others have of us, even though they're a novice.

It doesn't matter who it is: parents, siblings, partners, best friends, work colleagues; nobody has anywhere near the amount of information on ourselves as we do. We are always going to be the expert, and by comparison everyone else on this planet is a complete novice. Any attempt we make to modify ourselves to suit someone else's opinion is us saying, "Even though you're a novice, I'll take your opinion over mine, the expert."

This can lead to a tremendous amount of anxiety when we're trying to keep everyone happy, because we do something to keep that person happy, then we look over there and that's annoyed somebody else. We change to please them; somebody else gets annoyed.

We're never going to keep everyone happy.

The only person we need to actually

focus on keeping happy is our self.

The result of that is that we start to focus only on the things that we have direct control over.

Jon: You are the expert on you?

Tim: Exactly.

10. The last (and first) rule of anxiety control

Jon: Number 10.

Tim: Number 10. I call it the "last and first rule of controlling your anxiety."

Basically, it's about only concerning yourself with things that you have direct control over.

The things you have no control over: what other people do, what other people think, what challenges life is going to throw at you, what's going to go on in this world around you; you have no control over that. Yet, we spend a lot of time worrying ourselves about what might happen, what they might do, what might occur, what that person thinks about that. We don't have any control over that.

As a result, if we put our attention on

all the things we have no control over, then we recognise that all the things we perceive we are out of control of, and therefore we feel out of control of our life.

But if we choose to only put the focus on the things we have direct control over, then we feel in control of our life.

Those things are our own responses, our own reactions, our own emotions.

If all the work we do in terms of our processing and where we put our attention is concerned with us alone, then we look at the world and we see something that we have complete control over. *We control* the controllable and ignore the rest.

Mistakes, Myths and Misunderstandings to Avoid

Jon: Tim, what is the number one mistake anxiety sufferers make in the area of being able to control anxiety?

Tim: The biggest mistake people make is they try to *get rid of anxiety*.

Jon: Can you clarify it a little bit exactly what that is? What do you mean by that?

Tim: There's something that we operate on, a principle that is: that what we focus on grows. Wherever we put our focus becomes bigger to us. The same as we use a magnifying glass to zoom in and suddenly it takes up our whole vision.

What we focus on grows. If all we're

looking to do is stop feeling anxious, then we have to constantly be aware of what anxiety is, where it is, what causes it, and it has to be something that's very prevalent and in the forefront of our mind in our life.

Let me compare this to, let's say there was somebody I didn't want to be within 100 yards of in this world.

Never.

To achieve that, I have to know where they are at all times. 24 hours a day, seven days a week, I have to know where they are if I'm going to be more than 100 yards from them.

You can already see the amount of energy and effort I'm putting into thinking about this person that I don't want to be anywhere near.

The better strategy is to say, "Okay let's

work out where they never go. Then, if I go there, I know I'll never see them, and I can forget about them completely."

Rather than trying to get rid of anxiety, which means we have to focus on it all the time, let's move towards what is incompatible with anxiety: calm, confidence, happiness, positivity, enthusiasm; all the positive emotions that we know are going to just make us forget about the anxiety.

If we focus on going towards the good stuff, then before we know it we've left anxiety miles behind.

Jon: Why is that a mistake? Why do people make that?

Tim: I think because they're once again trying to eradicate anxiety completely. They're trying to live a life where they never feel it.

You wake up in the morning, and this is what anxiety sufferers do a great deal of, is self-scanning. They'll wake in the morning, they'll open their eyes, and they'll gauge where they are... have they got anxiety to a great degree; because they know it's going to dictate what they can do today, whether they feel anxious or not. You wake up; wherever you feel anxiety normally, you have a check for it.

Just by doing that, you create an anxiety response, because you're waiting for the result of this little assessment that you're doing on yourself.

That creates anxiety.

Suddenly, "Oh, I can feel anxiety." That thought, "I've got anxiety today," creates further anxiety, because that's an anxious thought. Before you know it, just by seeing if you've got it or not, you've created it and amplified it.

This is why people fall into the same mistakes all the time. **Anxiety goes when you stop paying it attention,** if that makes sense.

Jon: What they should do instead is what?

Tim: What people tend to do, I see them and I'll ask them what are they going to do when they haven't got this high-level anxiety anymore, and they tell me what they're going to do.

"I'm going to go for that jog," or, "I'm going to get back to work, because I've been off work with anxiety."

They're waiting to experience that feeling of feeling the way they did before they had high levels of anxiety. As a result, everything gets put on hold.

The actual best strategy is to get on with

your life; it's to say, "You know what? I'm going to decide to go back to work. I'm going to start that project anyway because I'm not going to let the anxiety dictate whether I'm able to or not."

I'm not saying it's an easy thing to do, because a bit of you is saying, "Yeah, but this is what stopped us doing it in the first place."

All the time we're waiting for anxiety to leave us we put our life on hold and we're just paying attention to it.

We're just giving it all of our time and all of our energy. As a result, it's sticking around.

If we just get on with our life, we'll get to the end of the day and we'll realise, "Oh, I didn't think about it at all. It didn't bother me at all."

As soon as we stop fearing it, it takes

away the power of that feeling.

Because guaranteed, if we gauge it again on a zero-to-10 scale, the high levels of anxiety, anything above five, only occurs generally, (as in elongated over a period of time), when we fear the feeling of anxiety.

We've got two or three out of 10 of the things that we're actually dealing with in our lives, and then the fear of anxiety adds on the extra five or six and creates it into that big thing that we simply can't deal with anymore.

As soon as we just say, "Right. I might feel anxious today. It will show me I'm alive, so that's fine. I'll get on with the day." We tend to just leave it behind.

Jon: What's the biggest myth? The world's full of social myths and we get more of them now. What's the biggest myth that most often causes anxiety sufferers to fail completely with their normal ... with their natural anxiety control.

Tim: The biggest myth I think that I encounter, and I bought into before I was doing this job that I do now, is that anxiety is effectively a terminal illness, that when you have been diagnosed with anxiety it is something that you will now simply be managing rather than leaving behind. I see that all the time.

The problem there is that as soon as you buy into that framework of, "I'm not meant to be getting out of this. I'm meant to just be tolerating it and tiptoeing my way around situations that cause it," then you're not trying to get out of it. Your subconscious mind doesn't waste its time trying to do things that are futile.

I don't spend a lot of time trying to learn to levitate, because you know I don't think I'm going to be able to.

When I was young and I first got a Rubik's cube, I tried it for a bit. I decided, "I can't solve this." Then I lost all enthusiasm for playing around with it anymore.

It was only when I discovered YouTube and the videos where they show you how to do it that I picked up my Rubik's cube and learned how to do it, because suddenly my mind's...

Jon: I've just got to say this. You are one of the fastest people at solving the Rubik's cube I know. Go on.

Tim: Again, I wouldn't have even attempted to get that good at it *if* I thought it was futile to try and do it.

All the time your mind says, "Well, I'm not looking for a solution to anxiety. I'm not looking to feel what I would regard as 'normal' because it's not an option for me; because somebody told me or I read something or a bit of literature suggested once I've got it I will always have it."

As soon as you buy into that myth, then your mind is not even trying to help you anymore.

Jon: Why is it a myth? Why do people supposedly in the know, why do they support it?

Tim: I wish I could answer that. You'd have to ask them that. I can only think because we have scans now that can tell you about there's a chemical imbalance that causes that.

The thing they don't seem to accept, that we ... again, I think it's because we come from the world of hypnotism where we change people's fears, habits, behaviours like that. We know we can update, we can upgrade.

Because we come from that framework, we realise it doesn't matter whether someone regards this as, "I was born with it," or whether someone regards it as, "something in my life now created this state of affairs in my head."

We know it is all changeable. It is all up-dateable and upgradeable. I don't necessarily think your general mental health practitioners understand it in that way.

I saw a bit of research that was on ... I can't remember what programme it was. They were saying about how they're considering using LSD and hallucinogens to deal with anxiety and depression.

They did a trial in America and they're now considering it as something that they would actually prescribe because of the 'astonishing' quality of the results. It was something like 50% to 60% of people studied, reported a general upturn in mood and experience of life.

They said then, "and it compares so favourably to psychoanalytical methods, that have a 51% success rate."

I thought to myself, "If I had a 51% success rate, I'd stop doing what I'm doing or I'd go and learn how to get better at it."

If I fall below 90% success rate for people I see for anxiety, then I'm thinking, "Whoa. I'm having a bad day here. I'm having a bad week. I need to hit the books or I need to get some rest or something like that."

Generally I think this is because their framework is, "You're going to do 6 sessions, 12 sessions; you're going to be with me for months, years maybe, and hopefully we'll work our way towards a solution." Then they're not expecting necessarily to be able to change this quickly.

We know we can, and it's all about the understanding of how your mind works, in my opinion.

Jon: If people are stuck in this myth, what should they do to fix it? How do you want to fix it? How do you want to get people out of it and get them thinking?

Tim: How I want to fix this? I want to educate people in exactly this model we understand and that seems to get these startlingly dynamic and speedy results.

I want them to understand it so they know it's an option. When I talk about dealing with people's issues and their subconscious patterns of thought, I have a very, very simple model in terms of how "therapy" occurs.

You have a pattern of thought that's going on that you don't like, and you recognise a pattern of thought you would rather have that would be much better for you.

Your subconscious mind is really, really good at updating. That's how it learns. When we were crawling around as a baby and we learned to walk on two feet, we didn't go back to crawling because we thought, "Hang on... this is easier on the knees... we're getting places a bit faster now."

We saw the shiny stuff and we updated it. Our mind went to it automatically. There was no intervention there. We just said, "I've learned something better. Let's do it."

The reason why your subconscious mind isn't updating your issues with

anxiety is because there are barriers
between *this* pattern that's bad, and *that*
pattern you know would be better.

These barriers take the form of
subconscious objections; reasons why,
"This looks good, but it ain't possible."

The biggest barrier that I experience
with my clients is the belief that,
"I am stuck this way. This is who I am.
This is how I operate, and I can't
change it."

Sometimes we take that barrier down
for them, we educate them, we let them
know it's possible. Their mind just
works it out, and it works out other
things as well.

You know, I'll use one of your stories
here about somebody you worked with
who had social anxiety and fear. You
got rid of the fear, and suddenly they

weren't afraid of heights anymore.

In my model of how that's working I'm saying you know what? Their crew members looked around at this crew member that's just done something different and said,
"Wait a minute. He's just done something different. Are we allowed to change what we're doing?"

Some of them worked it out and said, "Well, actually, I've been wanting to be better in this way before."

Now that barrier's not there. That barrier of belief that says, "I'm stuck like this." Suddenly we can do it.

The number of people I see, and especially on the workshops where we teach people to do this stuff for themselves, the people I see that change something on the day but then spontaneously something unexpected improves for them simply because their subconscious worked out change was possible.

That's what I want to change, is our understanding about how easily we can update.

Jon: What in your experience, because you said to me that you felt that nearly everything you see is anxiety-based anyway, what in your finding, in your experience ... and it's a vast experience now: seven years of seeing clients every day.

What's the number one misunderstanding that they have where they think in their minds they're actually doing the right thing and don't realise that it's a misunderstanding?

Tim: The biggest misunderstanding, and I hear this all the time: as soon as I explain to people about the crew members in there, and I'll say, "Because there's a crew member in there whose job it is to make you feel anxious to focus you on the thing that needs focusing on in its opinion", the number of times I hear people say, "Can we throw that crew member overboard? Can we get rid of it?"

That's the biggest misunderstanding is that this part of you is your enemy, when really it can be your *best friend*.

You'll see this. I see this on forums and Facebook and social media. You see people saying, "*My* anxiety is like this sack that arrives now and again and just jumps on me and stops me doing anything, and it hates me and it wants to make my life a misery."

That's the biggest misunderstanding, is that that part actually wants you to be unhappy. You've got to remember, it's a part of you. It's actually using anxiety in it's opinion as a strategy for happiness.

It's not looking to keep you down.

It's trying to keep you safe.

It's trying to make sure that you're paying attention to the things at the appropriate level so that you remain safe, and therefore can experience happiness in this world.

But what it's doing is a misunderstanding of where you are in your life right now.

The number of times we concern ourselves with things that might have been a concern for an infant but wouldn't necessarily be a concern for an adult; just because that crew member is doing the same job it was doing when we *were* an infant and keeping us safe as if we still *are*.

That's the biggest misunderstanding I think is that you actually have an enemy in there that's trying to keep you down.

5 point Massive Motivation

Jon: That brings us beautifully onto the final section, final chapter.

Can you give us, Tim, five top tips for changing things right now?

Before I put the book down, before they've stopped listening to the audio, before they stop watching the video, whichever way they're consuming this, the audience for this, can you tell them five things they can just do straight away?

Tim: **First thing...** is what we just said.

Don't treat anxiety as your *enemy*. Treat it as your **friend.**

I think if we look at this as it is, we have

a bit of us that's trying to keep us safe. It's trying to protect us, so it's not our enemy. It's actually our best friend. When you talk to yourself, when you're doing that self talk that says, "Why am I doing this? Why do I feel this way?"

Don't be angry with yourself. If you're angry with yourself, all you're doing is being angry with that crew member that's doing its best anyway.

You've got to treat it like the child that needs your reassurance.

Because you've got to remember this: that part of your subconscious, that member of your crew, is an uneducated child doing its best for you.

You've got to remember, you are the adult. You look at this situation. You say, "I shouldn't feel anxious about this. I shouldn't have this feeling. What can I

do to help this part change what
feelings its triggering for me?"

Because that part is the bit with its
fingers on the switches that can decide,
are you going to feel anxious or are you
going to feel happy?

Second thing... I want you to do: listen to
what the anxiety is telling you.

Listen to what it is regarding.

Because all the time you're trying to
shut it out, you're trying to push it away,
you're trying to ignore it, it's going to
shout louder.

You've got to pay attention to it on the
level that it's trying to communicate
with you, (as in there is something you
need to put your attention on).

This is why we get overwhelmed,

because everyone's shouting at once.

We've got to break it down to one thing at a time.

If it is a case of everyone shouting at once, do the one thing.

Pick one thing and do it. Take action, and that bit can sit down.

Do things one at a time. I can't recommend that highly enough.

Actually pay attention to what the anxiety is about rather than how it feels.

Thirdly... know with absolute certainty you are *not ill.*

I don't care. I don't give a shit if the doctor said to you, "You are ill. You have a disorder. You have a condition."

You don't.

You have **an emotion** that has got out of control in your eyes.

It has got to higher levels than you want it to get to.

You are not ill and you are certainly not stuck being ill.

You have to understand, anxiety is something to work with, not something to fear.

Fourthly... be kind to yourself in terms of rest and sleep. Allow yourself to get your rest.

If you're laying there awake at night pondering things, what will tend to happen then is you'll look at the clock, you'll say, "Right. It's 3AM now. If I go to sleep right now I'd only get four or five hours' sleep."

Then, before you know it, you look and it's 4AM.

The time that you can actually have to get to sleep is reducing and you're panicking. You're thinking, "Tomorrow I'm going to be exhausted. Tomorrow's going to be such a chore to me, so difficult for me."

If you're laying in bed and you're awake: you're resting. Just accept that.

As soon as you stop worrying about when you're going to get to sleep, guess what happens? You fall asleep. You've got to allow yourself to do this.

Because what you've done, you've created *cortisol* in your system, which is the *stress hormone*. As soon as you get anxious about, "How am I going to sleep?" You get stressed.

It fights against the natural melatonin

that you produce when it gets dark,
whose job it is to put you to sleep.

Stop fighting yourself. Just say,
"I might be awake all night, but that's
okay because I'm laying here doing
nothing, so at least I'm resting my body
and I'll feel better than I do right now,
in the morning."

The only reason we feel rubbish in the
morning through lack of sleep is
generally because we've been fretting
about it whilst it's been happening.

Allow yourself to get that sleep.

Finally... a kind word to yourself.

Just recognise you're doing really well.

Anxiety has a horrible tendency to make
you think that you're rubbish and that
you're not doing well at life.

Everyone feels anxiety and everyone at

some point allows anxiety to get to really high levels that aren't helping them, where they become very aware of the feeling rather than the situation they're in.

Just know that you're doing really well.

You've got this far in life. You're still alive.

Have a kind word for yourself on a daily basis.

These are my five things that I think **you can do straight away** that would radically change the way your body and your mind is responding towards the idea of anxiety.

Jon: Tim, Tim Box, thanks very much for that. I hope I'm not labouring the point, but I'm sure enough that our audience of anxiety sufferers and people who are interested in mental health, and of course anyone else who's reading this or listening to it or watching it, will no doubt be very interested in finding out even more from you.

Where do people find you mostly? Because it's a busy world, and you could be anywhere no doubt.

Tim: It is on the dreaded Internet that we've been talking about, obviously.

They can go to: ClearYourHeadBook.com to find out more about me.

That's the first port of call for them.

If you are suffering with anxiety and you want to actually be able to talk to somebody and become part of a group that are working together, we have the *Clear Your Head Facebook Group,* which is fairly easy to find.

I'm on Facebook as well. You could also stop by my website, which is: TheControlSystem.co.uk, which is where you can just find out a little bit more about me.

Jon: They can find out more from those.

Tim: Absolutely. Any of those sources.

They can pretty much talk directly to me as well.

Jon: If you are reading this as a book, there will be an ... there is an audio version somewhere. You will find out that there is going to be a video tutorial as we get feedback off the book. We're going to be doing a video tutorial and we'll be doing a Q&A on that, which will be rather exciting in answering all the questions.

On behalf of the Hypnoarts Publishers, Tim, thanks very much from the bottom of my heart for becoming one of our authors.

Tim: It's an absolute pleasure. Thank you so much for asking me. It's an honour.

Postword

Hi there, it's Jonathan Chase.

I'm incredibly lucky because as Director and Interviewer for HypnoArts Partnership Publishing, I'm allowed to be Midwife to some awesome people's ideas, expertise and treasures being shared with the world.

Tim Box is not only an erudite and enthusiastic people person and speaker, he is an innovative Creator, and an optimistic yet practical practitioner of his art of helping people think better.

As with all of the HypnoArts 'handbooks' Tim gifts his simple and life changing ideas with an ease and passion most of us would love to be able to do.

But, don't be fooled by his simplicity of approach. Tim's understanding of how anxiety works, and how to control that, surpasses the majority of thought and practice in the field today.

Often it is only when someone shakes away the leaves that we get to find the beans, and, in the case of Clear Your Head, actually get to discover that this approach does what it says on the tin.

If you suffer from an overwhelm of anxiety; if nothing else has helped; if you don't want chemicals and drugs to be your crutch, then Tim's subconscious style and coaching will show you how to get there. . . in control.

Envoi: This is a 'Postword'.

Unlike a foreword I'm not here to tell you to read the book; I'm here to tell you to read it again, and again.

As with all #HypnoArtsBooks you should be able to do that on an average commute into town, definitely while you're waiting for your cancelled flight, or over a couple of lunches.

Our authors don't do fluff or fancy passages full of rhetoric, we don't do the 'bigger the book the better the content' thing.

So go back and read it again. Make notes in the margins. Fold page corners to mark the best bits. Spill coffee and tea on the cover...

READ the book and allow it to help your life change.

Enhance Your Experience. Now.

HypnoArts™ Publications

Enhancing the Experience of Life

For the most up to date information on;
Books, Audio, Courses and Video Tutorials,
Author information, links to forums
and FaceBook groups Live Author Appearances and events
download the free #HypnoArts App
from iTunes App Store or Google Play

or Visit **HypnoArts.com**
and grab your copy of our email newsletter.

We look forward to meeting you.
Jane Bregazzi. CEO HypnoArts

Notes:

CPSIA information can be obtained
at www.ICGtesting.com
Printed in the USA
BVHW060821141222
654212BV00012B/1154

9 781999 764135